Abraham and his wife Sarah, had many sheep. They had herds of goats and fields of cattle and cute little pets to keep them company.

But they had NO children. Their friends had children, lots of them. But Abraham and Sarah didn't even have one to call their own.

One day God gave Abraham a message, "Pack up all your things and go to a land that I will show you. I will be your guide."

It was a little bit scary to leave home and travel to a land he had never been to before. It would be a long and uncomfortable trip.

But Abraham and Sarah trusted God and obeyed. They packed their things and prepared the animals for the journey.

Abraham walked and rested, and then walked some more. God said "Keep walking. You're almost there!" So they continued the journey.

Abraham didn't have a map. He didn't have a compass or even a GPS. But he had God as his guide.

Abraham, Sarah and their servants finally arrived. It was a beautiful place. God is the best guide and his surprise land was awesome.

They admired their new home. There was green grass for the animals, streams of water and fields to grow plenty of food.

Many years later, on a starry night, God spoke to Abraham and said; "I am all powerful and I have an even bigger surprise for you."

"I will give you a son. He will have children, and his children will have children, and they will have more children. And one day they will be as many as the stars in the sky."

Abraham laughed. "My wife and I are way too old to have children now." But Go
said, "I always keep my promises. You must agree to honor Me and obey Me."

Abraham decided it was best to listen to God, since He knows best. But many years passed without having children, and now they where even older.

One day God sent news to Abraham. Three men came to visit and said that Sarah was going to have a son in 9 months.

Sarah heard this and laughed. It had been years, and she was even older now, way too told to have a child. It was hard to believe.

There are two things that we can be sure of; That God loves us and that God is good. And sure enough, Sarah soon realized that she was pregnant. Amazing!

God's promise came true after all, and Sarah had a baby boy. They named him Isaac, which means "laughter". That's because Isaac brought them much joy and laughter.

Sometimes people are mean and they hurt each other. And that's what all the people were doing in 2 cities not too far from where Abraham lived.

But God wants to keep His children safe. He sent the same visitors to get Abraham's cousin Lot, and family out before the cities were destroyed.

Sometimes it is hard to know why God does some things. Abraham didn't always understand either. But God can't do anything bad. He wanted Abraham to be so sure of this, so He gave him a test.

"Abraham, I want you to give Me back your son, Isaac." God said. "What? You are asking me to give my only son? Isaac that I waited for, for so long?" Abraham asked.

But Abraham knew that God was loving and good. He trusted God before and everything went well. Difficult as it was, he decided to obey God's request.

Abraham once again obeyed God. God told him; "You have passed the test. And now, you may keep Isaac. Through him, I will continue to fulfill my promise to you!"

In the Bible, Abraham shows us many examples of faith and trusting God. Can you think of other ways you can practice faith in your daily life?

iCHARACTER

Published by iCharacter Ltd. (Ireland)
www.icharacter.org
By Agnes and Salem de Bezenac
Illustrated by Agnes de Bezenac
Copyright 2015. All rights reserved.

Copyright © 2015 by iCharacter Ltd.. All rights reserved. No part of this book may be reproduced in any form or by any electronic or mechanical means, including information storage and retrieval systems, without written permission from the publisher or author, except in the case of a reviewer, who may quote brief passages embodied in critical articles or in a review.

www.ingramcontent.com/pod-product-compliance
Lightning Source LLC
Chambersburg PA
CBHW081503070526
44586CB00019B/2464